HOW TO:
STOP DATING & BE IN AN EFFORTLESS, COMMITTED RELATIONSHIP

BY MICHELLE CHUNG

Book Cover by Michelle Chung
Edition Number 4, 2023

Michelle Chung
Barcelona, Spain
www.michellechungcoach.com

'After years of searching for my soulmate, I finally found the person, I have always dreamed of! Big thanks to Michelle and her coaching sessions, which guided me to where I was supposed to go and gave me the feeling of safety and strength which I needed to apply on this journey, highly recommend her expertise 100%!'

Claudia Alkin
Austria

'I have a great life, a wonderful successful career, what's missing is a partner to share it with. I was really stuck on attracting this person into my life, so I worked with Michelle to really get clear on what were the blocks keeping this person from coming into my life, I had a lot of beliefs around, "he doesn't exist, he won't want me, we are not going to meet each other" and a whole bunch of other things she helped me to clear, and also I didn't have a clear vision of what he was like, what we were like together, and what our life was like, so we really worked to clear the blocks and a clear vision, and it gave me something I haven't had in a really long time regarding a partner, is HOPE and possibility that he actually exists, and that it will happen, it gave me a sense of security and peace that I carry each day with me, and Michelle was key and instrumental in helping me get this clarity and hope, So I recommend working with Michelle, she has a really nice coaching style that helps you bring forth what is best in you, and I can't recommend her enough, it has been very helpful to me and I know he is on his way! Thanks!'

Dr Kyrin Dunston MD
USA

'I loved working with Michelle, always felt so comfortable in our sessions. She helped me overcome some mindset blocks in my career and personal life. I had already read all the self-help and coaching books, but I needed something more personalised. Together we identified what was holding me back and what I really had to change and grow in my career and personal life. I 100% recommend her and know I will continue to use her coaching services.'

Paulina Camizao
Mexico

'Michelle's coaching is so inspiring! I leave her sessions feeling totally recalibrated. She has an amazing way of bringing practicality into the relationship and love sphere, which is so important for someone like me. After feeling burnt out from bad dating and career experiences for a couple of years, I've been following Michelle's guidance and I feel way more set to take on everything I've been putting off doing. Very grateful'

Chelsea Joy
UK

"Working with Michelle has brought so much peace and clarity in my life. She helped me clear self limiting beliefs and self judgement which was holding me back from being my true self and achieving higher levels of success. In finding my why/purpose, it's improved my relationship to my business and I've been able to turn around negative situations to great success"

Katrina Lee
Australia

PROLOGUE

This book is for women who run a business or are in a high level position in their careers and don't want to date the 'regular' way - online, constantly going to meet ups, networking events in the hope they will 'meet someone special'.

This is not written for people who want someone to kill time with, a casual, short-term relationship or a warm body for winter, and will settle for just anyone in order not to be alone.

This book is written for assertive, ambitious women with a mission, who are seeking to make an impact on the world through their work and desire love, support and growth along the journey of life, and find an equally intelligent, emotionally mature, secure man to walk that journey with.

This book will show you the most effective way to attract the right man who aligns with your values, your goals and your lifestyle, who also values freedom and has the same vision for their future as you do.

You're probably quite successful in everything you do in life, but love and relationships may be an area where you haven't succeeded in the way you would have liked.

You may be divorced, or single for more than 4-5 years, and have found it really difficult to find someone you would consider an equal or who really 'gets' you.

People describe you as strong, confident, successful, are really good in your role or running your business, and seem to have it all, but are starting to get worried about you as you get older because you haven't found a partner you can 'settle down' with.

But your friends and family who really know you, know that you are actually just self-assured and driven to help people around you, a natural born leader amongst your friends and colleagues and often take care of everyone around you more than you take care of yourself.

You seem to have a tough, strong exterior, a natural born leader since you were a kid, but on the inside you just want love and to be cared for and not have to lead and decide everything all the time, and you're a lot softer than you come across. .

You want to be more vulnerable and not get hurt, because in the past you thought vulnerability was a weakness, but now you recognise you need to open up and let people see the real you.

You are more emotionally mature and conscious than the people around you, so your quiet self-knowing may come across as self confident, but never in an aggressive way, and men AND women are drawn to you because of your natural leadership and nurturing personality.

Men want to be in a relationship with you, they may see you as a challenge, having a smart and independent partner is highly desirable for most guys, but often an imbalance of power ruins the relationship, as men may have tried to diminish your light, tone down your genius because they are intimidated by your natural shininess and success.

Other problems you may have had in the past with your ex partner - when he started becoming more passive and you needed him to step up and be a leader too, but he either didn't have it in him or wasn't ready to grow with you.

You may get easily stressed and overwhelmed because you naturally take on the responsibilities that few step up for, leading others around you constantly, in a collaborative way, never in an autocratic or forceful way, but sometimes it can be really lonely, and you want a partner who understands this and supports you!

You are bright, brilliant and fun, love going to restaurants and being in a cosmopolitan vibe, with inspiring, caring friends around you, but you also balance it out with self care, mental and emotional wellbeing by being out in nature, exercise and fitness and having some time to yourself.

But maybe you don't look after yourself enough, preferring to fill up your calendar with lots of activities so you don't feel the lull of loneliness and being confronted with what's missing in your life - the partner who is equal or even can be your teacher and inspiration, and learn and grow from each other together, instead of always giving and pouring from your cup.

This book will help you understand yourself better, how to attract a strong, supportive, highly emotionally intelligent and financially stable man, so you can continue your good work inspiring and leading people around you, because you deserve love and support too.

ACKNOWLEDGEMENT

This book is dedicated to the amazing women and men out there looking for love, who are brave enough to follow your path and make the world a better place!

I was also in the same place as you may be in right now, single, dating, or tired of dating, or not had the time or interest to do date...

But wanting someone special to share your life with, walk the journey together and grow together.

I'm so fortunate and grateful to have met my partner Raf Adams in 2021, my soul-mate, my inspiration, my guide, my love! You give my work and my vision new insight and new energy, and walking this entrepreneur road is no longer lonely or an uphill battle.

Thanks to my family, especially mum Imelda who showed me how to be a strong woman but also how to be a respectful and loving wife and mother, dad Johnny who always supported me to do whatever career and business I chose, and my brother Eugene who has inspired me as he has grown into an amazing husband and dad to wife Laura, and my nephews Jasper and Remy!

CONTENTS

CHAPTER 1. HOW TO FIGURE OUT WHAT YOU REALLY WANT IN A RELATIONSHIP

I guess I have been blessed with a variety of relationships, from short-term teenage relationships, to longer ones over a few years, to being married, then divorced and back to single again.

I had a 'regular' childhood, with immigrant parents who are still together after 43 years, we moved to Australia from Asia when I was 3 years old, with my older brother of only 18 months.

But I always felt lonely growing up, my friends always lived quite far away and because I had moved houses several times, I didn't know the kids in my neighbourhoods and going to an all-girls high school far away from home meant that I had even less contact or opportunity to talk to boys!

I used to think ...

"IT MUST BE SUCH A RARE COINCIDENCE TO FIND SOMEONE WHO LIKES YOU BACK!"

When I was 20, I once asked my gay friend Antonio - when did you first know you were gay? And he said 'you know in primary school, when you liked boys? I liked boys too!'

During your childhood, you start to acknowledge what you want, you start to develop feelings for the boys or girls in your school, and you don't know why you like them, you just know that you do!

When you're a kid, you just know what you like, and a lot of kids have the courage and lack of self-judgement most adults don't - they innocently and directly tell their crush they like them!

THE EX-BOYFRIEND #1

My first 'real' relationship was with a guy who was much older than I was, I was working a part time job at a classical music venue during university in Sydney and he worked there too.

It was the kind of job that many actors, musicians and creatives took on, so they could have a flexible schedule.

He was the new hot guy that started, a friend of the manager, a part time DJ, gym trainer... and at that age, every girl wants a muscly, DJ boyfriend right?

I didn't pay that much attention to him, I was 19, naive and awkward and couldn't understand how anyone would be attracted to me, I didn't wear makeup and was never one of the 'cool kids' at work or even at school.

I couldn't believe it when he started showing interest in me, and I was very surprised to discover that we had a very deep soul connection, I felt like I could see right into him and he into me, like he just 'got' me so easily and effortlessly.

The relationship wasn't without its issues and disagreements, the major one being that he was in his early 30's and wanted to have a family ASAP, and didn't see the relationship continuing because he didn't want to limit my options in life.

So after 3 months of a very easygoing, exciting and intense relationship, we broke up and I was devastated.

"SCHOOL TEACHES YOU THE LESSON FIRST & THEN YOU DO THE TEST. LIFE GIVES YOU THE TEST FIRST, AND THEN YOU MUST RECOGNISE THE LESSON"

If you really want to change the way you do things, you must reflect and analyse your past experiences, or you will remain unconscious and doomed to repeat it again.

Awareness is the key for true change.

This first serious relationship showed me that meeting someone and being in a relationship could be easy, effortless and there was definitely someone out there who 'got' me.

I rebelled from my parents, they were shocked to know I was seeing someone so much older, and that I wasn't their little girl anymore.

I discovered that I was someone worthy of love and attention, and the relationship taught me to just be myself, and it was totally ok to be authentically myself.

I also learned the heartache of a breakup, how it was to love someone, how it was to let go and grieve the loss of a great relationship.

THE EX-BOYFRIEND #2

My next relationship was a guy from university, when I studied Industrial Design at the University of Technology, Sydney from 1999-2003.

Again, it was an effortless and easy relationship, I was not looking for anyone, and we fell into it quite quickly.

I remember asking my gay friend Antonio what he thought of this new guy, and he thought he was pretty cute, so I just went with his seal of approval.

It was a pretty smooth relationship, hardly any fights or problems, we were in our early 20s and were keen to work full time, and also travel around the world in our holidays.

But eventually after 3.5 years together, I realised that I wanted more, I was grateful to be in a comfortable relationship with a very smart, generous and kind guy, but I always felt like I wanted to do more with my life, I just wasn't sure what it was.

At around the same time, when I was 26 I started training Capoeira, a Brazilian martial art street sport, and I was inspired by the acrobatic movement, energy and amazing community of people like myself, in our mid 20s and early 30s, enjoying the Sydney lifestyle and beaches, working in our jobs during the day and in the evenings and weekends being part of this amazing vibrant group of people living life to the fullest.

I started seeing a different side to myself, a more empowered, extroverted me, letting go of the shy, awkward and naive person I was during school and my early 20's.

And eventually my relationship couldn't keep up, he said he started feeling left out, and that I wasn't coming to watch him at his soccer practice anymore.

I was outgrowing him.

All breakups are sad, even if you are the one instigating it.

I really thought he would be the one I would have married, had a family when I hit 30 and live in that big house with the picket fence and soccer games on the weekends.

But that wasn't for me!

What I learned from this relationship was how lovely his family were, that a nice comfortable routine and lifestyle were great but after a while I was craving growth and wanted to live into the extroverted part of me - I wanted to do much more with my life, to travel, start businesses and really experience the best life had to offer.

One experience that stood out clearly in this relationship, was when I asked him 'what do you want to do' and he said 'anything you want to'... and this really made me realise - I wanted a man who was also a leader, could make decisions and guide our relationship towards SOMEWHERE, and that I didn't want to have to make all the decisions ALL the time.

I didn't know it at the time, but I had a lot more masculine traits and natural leadership than he did, and it started to exhaust me, wanting him to be more masculine so I didn't have to be.

In hindsight, I now recognise he had a much more gentle, feminine personality than I did, and I got bored and eventually wanted something and someone else.

THE EX-HUSBAND #1

It was not long after I broke up with my university boyfriend, that another love interest came into the picture.

Again, I was not looking for a relationship, and I was only single for a few months when one of the Instructors from my Capoeira academy let me know he liked me.

We had been in the same friendship group for a year, and he was also in a relationship with someone else, but when he found out I was single, he asked me out and said he wanted to break up with his girlfriend.

He was street smart and emotionally mature for his age, his parents splitting up when he was in his teens, and having to be the 'man' of the family at the age of 19, with 2 younger siblings and a mother who wasn't capable of looking after the kids or even herself.

We instantly 'got' each other and again, it was effortless, easy and fun to be in a relationship together. The years flew by quickly and eventually we were in that age of our early 30s when all our friends were getting engaged and married and thinking about kids and families.

We were really into financial freedom and at that stage I had started my own footwear design and manufacturing business and we had used the government grant to buy our first apartments and as he was a carpenter, and I was a designer, we had a lot of fun renovating them together.

We didn't want to spend a lot of money on a big white wedding, and my parents were tired of pushing us to get married, so eventually my dad suggested we get married in Vegas, while we were taking a gap year off work and travelling around the world.

And so one weekend when we were staying at my cousin's place in California, we decided to head to Las Vegas and get married!

We ordered some titanium rings from Amazon and hired a chapel and an Elvis impersonator (although I wanted Michael Jackson, it was Sunday and no one else was available), and we only had a few people there, my cousin, his wife and their kids.

We were completely unattached to any traditional sense of a wedding, or the ritual or sacredness of any of it, we just felt a pressure from my family to get married and move into the next phase of our lives everyone else was going through.

And then around 2013 a few years into our marriage, I started getting back injuries, after training Capoeira intensively for the last few years and luckily had escaped any major injuries so far.

I believed in Accupuncture and natural therapies and intuitively believe we can heal ourselves naturally.

After a few re-injuries, the acupuncture didn't give me any relief anymore, and my boss at the time (I was a designer for a famous homewares and kitchenware brand in Sydney), suggested I try Kinesiology.

I became fascinated and obsessed with the subject of natural healing, as I loved learning new things, and also for survival, because at this point I couldn't walk due to the sciatic pain. I was avoiding painkillers as much as possible but some days it wasn't possible to leave the house without them.

Some nights I would wake up and lie flat on the floor in chronic pain, and no doctors knew what to do.

I spent all my spare time online, research solutions to heal myself, why was I in chronic pain and how could I fix this.

Eventually I had to quit my full time job, because I was going to so many kinesiology and chiropractic appointments I didn't think it was fair to my boss, who had been really understanding and kind.

One weekend I went my good friend Rhonda's birthday party and one of her good friends mentioned she was taking a year off to study Reiki Healing.

It was such a revelation to me - taking a year off work to study as a mature age student!

And I thought to myself - why not?

We were 30, most of us were climbing the corporate ladder in some way or another, working hard, going to the gym, doing yoga, going out to restaurants and bars with friends in the evenings and weekends and life was normal.

Except for me with this massive, unrelenting chronic pain, unable to walk for a total of 12 months.

After I quit that design job, I decided to take the year off to study natural medicine, mostly to heal myself, and potentially a new career path.

It was so great to be a student again, and I always felt like mature-aged students always got more benefit and took things much more seriously than fresh-out-school teenagers did.

I did a double diploma of Kinesiology and Mind Body Medicine.

I learned how to listen to my body, to my intuition, to my inner voice.

It was the key to helping me heal my body and this chronic pain I had already endured for 6 months.

And it was the key to the end of my marriage too.

I remember I was practicing with my classmate Leah, we had become good friends and she was over at my place while my husband was at work.

She had given me a healing session and I clearly remember being so connected with my inner self, so clear about what I needed to do - there was no fear, no judgement or trying to rationalise it, it just felt like such pure inner wisdom and my intuition guiding me.

I got up from that session and distinctly remembered thinking to myself:

"I DON'T WANT TO BE IN THIS RELATIONSHIP ANYMORE"

It didn't make any sense, we had a great relationship together, we lived in an amazing part of the inner city Sydney, close to shops, restaurants, bars, universities, a wonderful park across the road with an outdoor pool - a great lifestyle, a comfortable marriage, we had enough money and work and everything was technically 'perfect'.

Except my body was not working the way it was supposed to.

We had even tried having kids, and had been trying since we had got married, but were disappointed every month with no result.

The next day after the healing session with Leah, 'coincidentally' I had an appointment with local the fertility clinic.

During the appointment, I sat there and just burst into tears, saying I didn't want to go ahead with the IVF treatment.

My husband was really confused, asking why we went to the appointment if I had already decided.

Pretty quickly I decided to tell my husband what my intuition told me from the healing session.

He was in shock, it was a shock to myself too, I hadn't even had time to process it myself.

The clues started adding up quietly in the background, but as there was nothing really obviously 'wrong' with our relationship, it came as a huge shock to my husband, and to all our friends and family.

My mum was in denial, wailing and crying and she couldn't understand why I would want to leave a perfectly good marriage.

My husband was a great guy, stable, loving, kind, funny, but he just wanted a comfortable and secure lifestyle, have a steady job, go to the gym, rinse, repeat. I wanted so much more, and our life vision was not the same. I had grown up with entrepreneurial, migrant parents and had been given every comfort and stability growing up, so all I wanted to do was spread my wings, but he wanted to stay roosting at home.

When I started doing Landmark Education programs, he said he felt like he was holding me back, when all I wanted to do was share it with him and go on a new journey together.

He didn't want to go on that journey, he was either happy where he was on wanted to go on a different journey, a more religious path.

I realised again, that I had repeated the cycle, in a relationship with someone I loved, but it was not the right path for me, I wasn't meant to be hiding in a 'normal' relationship, I was meant to reach my fullest potential, helping people, making an impact and leaving my mark on the world.

The extent of the back problems and sciatic pain literally stopped me in my tracks, and I realised that I was not living the life I was meant to be living.

In TCM (Traditional Chinese Medicine), they say that the cause of pain in your body is due to stagnation, and that the major cause of stagnation is not living in your flow, or not following your life purpose.

Dis-ease is a major sign that your life is not in alignment with your true purpose, what you were born on Earth to do.

Throughout the 12 months of chronic pain I had suffered, it caused me to literally stop and think, instead of going from situation to situation, falling into things, instead listening to what my soul was trying to tell me and make choices aligned to my purpose.

I believe we decide what we want to do, before we were born, and our journey on this planet is to rediscover what that plan was, and to live it.

The title of this chapter is about knowing what you want, and I think that's actually one of the hardest things in life!

And you can only do that through experiencing different relationships, different partners, although traditional marriage encourages you to have just 1 partner, I believe our purpose is to meet different people along your life journey so they can teach you something about yourself.

Knowing what you want, through a process of elimination, is one of the best ways to discover this, but the key is to STOP, REFLECT and think.

My personality was of action, fast decision-making and I would move on too quickly, to avoid the pain of looking within, to understand the real lesson I needed to understand.

PHYSICAL PAIN, ILLNESS AND DISCOMFORT IS YOUR SOUL'S WAY OF GIVING YOU A BIG WAKE UP CALL, A MASSIVE SIGNAL TO STOP AND LISTEN FOR THE RIGHT PATH.

I never once regretted my decision to separate and get divorced.

I trusted my intuition and it felt like the right thing, even though my family and friends couldn't believe it, and some congratulated me for being so courageous and brave, to split up and become single again.

For my parents it was a bit of cultural shame, a daughter divorced in her 30's, but I didn't care.

I had always followed my own decisions in life, call it stubborn, strong willed whatever... I knew I couldn't live the perfect life for them, or I would be miserable.

BEING SINGLE IN YOUR 30'S

Being single again at the age of 35, after 8.5 years in a relationship and being married, being hardly ever a day or week apart for that whole time, thinking this would be my 'til death do us part' relationship... it was a huge shock!

Being single again was not easy, especially after being in a relationship for nearly a decade.

I had more time to myself and realised the loneliness from childhood had not gone away. Being single in my 30's was a whole different game than being single in your 20's prior to technology, the internet, smart phones and online dating apps.

Never one to shy away from a challenge and hide away for too long, I downloaded Tinder and eventually a few other different dating apps, to try them out, but subconsciously I was just trying to avoid being alone.

It was fun at first, the dopamine rush, the feeling of being special, when you hear that particular ring of a dating app, you know which apps people are using by the sound that rings from their phones!

All of a sudden I was out in the world, exploring and experimenting what my boundaries were, completely unaware of what I was doing, just taking lots of actions and not thinking too far ahead.

Then one day, in 2016, I saw a Facebook ad for a digital nomad travel program, it was a way of travelling around the world safely, with a community of other remote working professionals ranging in age from their 20s-60s.

I thought this would be a good way to grow, see the world and perhaps meet someone along the way!

I interviewed for the 12 month program, which included an itinerary of 6 months in Europe, and 6 months in Latin America. I had always wanted to travel to LatAm but didn't want to travel alone.

This was the perfect next step for me, to change my environment, away from all my good friends from school and university that were having babies and talking only about stuff I was completely not aligned with anymore. I wanted to have a family, but I needed to find a partner first, and perhaps doing this travel program, I could meet someone that I was not finding in Sydney.

In March 2017, I landed in Split, Croatia, to meet my new community, a group of 40+ people from all over the world, mainly from the USA, some from Canada, Uk, another 2 fellow Australians and others from Europe and LatAm.

It was an interesting 'gap year' for me, it felt like I was in high school again!

If you hadn't sorted yourself out before, you would be completely confronted by it during this program!

I had completed several Landmark Education personal development programs (including being a coach on the Self Expression & Leadership Program) towards the end of my marriage, and thought I had enough tools to deal with all the personal and professional situations during the 2017 digital nomad program.

I hadn't realised that personal growth is a lifelong journey, I thought I had 'fixed' myself and I wouldn't be challenged again!

After a month in Split, our group travelled and lived a month each time in a different city - in Lisbon Portugal, Sofia Bulgaria, Belgrade Serbia, Valencia Spain, then over to LatAm starting in Buenos Aires and Cordoba Argentina, Lima Peru, Bogota and Medellin in Colombia and finished our program in Mexico (if you're interested in travelling in this same program, please check out my referral link www.remoteyear.com/general-application?referee=100235151

A few friends and clients have joined the programs after hearing my stories and you will love it if you're looking to travel, have a sea change and fresh new perspective for your life).

I was actively searching for my life partner while I was living in different cities, and met some amazing guys, but as soon as they knew I would be only there for a month, most lost interest and we kept things fun and casual, hoping to find a spark that maybe I could revisit after my program ended.

Travelling as a digital nomad for 12 months, working remotely, with a nomad community was eye opening and incredible experience I will never forget, because it led me to my next step.

AN IMPORTANT SEA-CHANGE

Not long after I got back to Sydney and began life yet again, did I hear one of the other members of the nomad group mention a Digital nomad Visa for Barcelona, Spain.

Something about that instantly piqued my interest, as I was considering relocating to Europe, to set up a base somewhere and be able to explore the other parts of Europe quickly and easily, while working remotely in my freelance design work.

And so when my friend mentioned Barcelona with it's nomad visa, my intuition told me it was the right thing to do

I only had 3 criteria really - beaches, bachata dancing and sun!

How did I know it was my intuition guiding me?

Because the messages always came from simple commands like 'do it', from somewhere in my torso area, and never from my head, where my logical brain was doing all the overthinking.

Finally after about 6 months of annoying bureaucracy with the Spanish office in Sydney, I got my visa approved, to live in Spain for 1 year, and I wrestled with my mind if I should go or not.

I had already built a community of great friends who were in the same boat as I was - single, in our mid 30s, loving life and hanging out like the 90's tv series Friends.

But my visa would expire if I didn't go, so I decided to leave just after my birthday in February, and arrived in Barcelona on the 13th February 2019.

A MESSAGE FROM THE UNIVERSE

Before I left, I threw a huge farewell party, with over 70 friends and family attending, and one particular friend, from my Kinesiology and Mind Body Medicine course was a gifted psychic healer.

Eve told me that in my future I would have 2 kids with a tall man with light hair and light eyes, and we would have them before we got married.

After my divorce I had vowed never to marry again, in my opinion it was not necessary to have the official paperwork etc or worth it either!

I didn't give this too much thought, as my dating life after my divorce had been pretty much like a hamster wheel, not meeting the right guy, going on endless tinder, bumble, hinge and other dating app dates that amounted to nothing close to the serious relationships I had had in the past.

In Barcelona I felt like I had a whole new life ahead of me, the sea change I had probably intuitively wanted.

I always found that changing my environment always gave me a fresh perspective on life, and suddenly I was in a foreign country, on the other side of the world, didn't know how to speak spanish and didn't really know what I was doing or what would happen to me.

But it felt like the right thing to do.

I never once doubted this decision, just like my decision to get divorced, I never regretted or doubted that decision either.

I realised that following my intuition always guided me to the right place, the right people, and the right path in my life and healed me in more ways than I could predict.

During my first year in Barcelona, I did an intensive 6 week spanish course, to relearn any spanish I had left after 6 months in LatAm and 11 months back in Sydney - all my spanish had disappeared!

And during the spanish classes, I met an awesome Brazilian fine artist, covered in tattoos and the most crazy fashion sense so of course we hit it off straight away!

He told me that he was studying at the Barcelona Academy of Art, and I had always struggled with my path of being an artist as a career since high school, as I chose a career in Industrial design instead because I thought I wouldn't make any money as an artist.

So here was my chance to try out my art career again.

Again, I was a full-time student again, and working part time as a freelance designer for my clients back in Sydney.

It was a dream lifestyle, met amazing, interesting people and drawing and painting every day was something I hadn't done in a very long time.

BOYFRIEND #3

In my first year in Spain, I met a great Spanish guy and we started dating casually for 8 months, he was also a part time artist and worked at a local gym as a fitness trainer. He was very attractive and kind and it was such a big change to the rollercoaster of mini-relationships during my digital nomad year.

And then in March 2020, things changed.

The Covid Lockdown in Barcelona was announced and within a few days, we were told we would not be able to leave our homes due to the virus spreading into Spain from Asia and other European countries.

I was literally homeless, I had just finished my first 12 month lease and my flatmate moved back home, and I had planned to fly back to Sydney for the birth of my first nephew, my older brother's son.

I had been staying with Evelina, a very kind friend from school who had kindly let me stay with her while I was waiting for my flight back to Australia.

When the lockdown was announced, my Spanish boyfriend invited me to stay with him, he had a 3 bedroom apartment, 2 cats and a balcony full of plants, as well as an art studio at home, so it was a no brainer! Evelina's place was also too tiny to have 2 people staying there 24/7 so I left to stay with him, thinking it would be just the weekend or a week max...

Little did I know, the 24/7 Covid lockdown in Barcelona lasted for 2 months!

It all went quite well, given that we had never lived together prior to that, we had a cozy little domesticated relationship and got along quite well.

During the lockdown, I saw an email from my real estate agent, it was a webinar about property, and I was a little resistant to too much online content, but my intuition kicked in again, a voice inside my body clearly said 'do it!'

The presenter of that real estate webinar was intriguing and I wanted to know more about her, so I interviewed her and it turned out she was also a life coach!

I immediately hired her, because I knew I needed help - to sort out a new career direction, find somewhere to live, and figure out what I would do next in my life.

I started working with her and realised I wanted to be a life coach - or at least change my career in the direction of personal growth and development, a path I had started to take towards the end of my marriage when I was doing Landmark Education courses and coaching.

I trained and certified as a life coach during the lockdown, and felt like I was finally on a wonderful new career path in my life.

The next thing I already knew intuitively was my relationship with my Spanish boyfriend.

We both knew that I needed someone much more ambitious than he was, and I felt like it was the perfect relationship for someone else who was NOT me, who deserved a stable, committed relationship. He was a great guy but I knew that if I decided to stay in the relationship, I would end up unhappy, unfulfilled and repeating the cycle with my ex-husband, I still wanted to reach my greatest potential and help people with my work, and I wanted a partner who was also entrepreneurial and could understand and support this kind of mindset.

After the lockdown ended, I moved into an AirBnb near the beach in Barcelona, it was the first time I had my own place since I arrived in Barcelona, and I was back to being alone again.

During this time I worked intensively with my life coach, she helped me to get clear and make decisions about my new business direction, find a permanent apartment in a place I loved, with an amazing view and feeling of abundance, lots of natural light and great energy.

I was also listening to a lot of business mentors, doing their coaching programs and listening to their podcasts.

ONE MENTOR SAID THAT IF I WASN'T GETTING THE RESULTS I WANTED, I WAS 'RESISTING' SOMETHING

I wasn't NOT meeting the right one because I WASN'T putting myself out there, I was busy working the dating apps, and meeting people live, in fact I was creating meetup groups and was the admin of one Barcelona Digital nomads and entrepreneurs group... so lack of meeting people was not the problem.

I took this advice pretty seriously, and kept thinking and pondering upon this, what was really blocking me?

I'm going to share the exact steps I did to stop dating (I had been on the dating scene for 5 years in a row!) and finally be in an effortless, amazing, committed relationship with my current partner (also an executive coach, author and speaker!).

I'll share these steps throughout this book, so make sure you watch out for them and highlight them:

STEP #1

All my study about the subconscious mind and manifestation, and there was still something I wasn't seeing, something that was blocking me from meeting the right person.

Find a quiet place and time to sit and be with yourself

Ask yourself

1. 'What am I resisting?'
2. 'What am I not seeing?'
3. 'What do I need to know?'

And wait for your subconscious mind to respond.

You need to keep asking yourself these questions, and then keep asking why, until you get to the real subconscious answer, because the first answer you get will be the rational, logical mind doing it's usual thing, those conversations you have in your head, the overthinking and overanalysing situations... you need to ask again 'why' at least 3 times, like a child, until the answer is probably something you haven't recognised before

I did this exercise with one coaching client, an attractive doctor in her mid 50's with 2 six figure online businesses, and I asked her to do this on her own, and we would discuss what she discovered in our next coaching call.

She turned up at the next session not having done it.

She said 'Oh, I'm not resisting anything' and I said, ok let's try it anyway.

It turned out her resistance was blocking her from meeting the right man, because her subconscious fear of ending up in the same kind of relationship as she had with her ex-husband, where she felt trapped and wanted freedom to do as she pleased.

She released all these old fears and emotions with an outpouring of tears, and afterwards she said she felt much lighter and felt like she was now ready to find someone.

She joined the digital nomad program I had done, as she had always wanted to travel to Africa, and was attracted to black men.

Six months later she contacted me, apologising for being AWOL and told me that she had fallen in love with a young man in Nairobi, the most mature and intelligent man she has ever met, even though their relationship was not without challenges, but she was in a relationship and she was happy!

So as you can see, if you have these subconscious blocks, you will keep yourself safe and sabotage yourself by not meeting, and not seeing the people with the potential to be your life partner.

Another woman I worked with, she had been single for several years. She was in her late 30's, beautiful, sporty, successful in her job at a well known multinational tech company and was a part-time fitness trainer, and was constantly on dating apps and each time we would meet she had a different love story with a bad ending.

When we did the resistance exercise together, she recognised that her subconscious block was also resisting falling back into the same relationship as her ex-boyfriend, because in that relationship she always felt guilty. She also recognised that her past long term relationships were always so much hard work and didn't know that effortless, easy and fun relationships actually existed!

I did these exercises and some personal manifestation work and within 3 months I met my current partner Raf Adams, through a meetup on Personal Growth and Spirituality book Club, to discuss books on business, personal development and spirituality I had started in August 2020, with the intention of attracting other conscious, spiritual entrepreneurs like myself.

Just after my birthday in February 2021, I got Covid! I asked my friend Francesco, who was in town visiting for a few months, to host my meetup group for me.

He was happy to do it, and reported back to me later, that an interesting guy had turned up - he was also a coach, and that I should meet him when I was recovered from Covid.

We connected in the Meetup group chat and I had a small idea that he might be interesting, but at that point, I had been meeting dozens and dozens of new people all the time, everyone was desperate to get out and meet new people after the strict Spanish 2 month lockdown, and subsequent re-lockdowns.

When we finally met, when I laid eyes on him, Raf was lying on the sand in his motorcycle jacket, in the group circle of my Saturday morning meetup group at the beach in Barcelona, I knew he was the one I had been waiting for.

SOUNDS CLICHE BUT WE JUST HIT IT OFF INSTANTLY...

He was a good foot taller than me, had light hair and light eyes, I couldn't tell if they were blue, green or grey, and later found out there was a dutch word for that perfect mix of those colours and it translated to something like apple sea green blue.

After the meetup group, we went to get some burgers at the local beach cafes, and he decided to come sit at the smaller table, at the the empty spot next to me.

We talked about coaching, and I discovered he was an executive coach, had lived in China for 12 years and also spoke Mandarin and Dutch, and he was from the Flemish part (north) of Belgium, and had written and published a few books called the Suited Monk www.suitedmonk.com - about the Life Journey, and how to bridge the gap between your Suit (external world) and your Monk (your internal world, intuition, life purpose).

Everyone from the meetup had been hanging out all afternoon and we found ourselves the last ones left!

He lived outside of Barcelona, and we had all planned to meet again for drinks later that evening, and I felt bad for him having to go all the way home and back again into town, so I invited him to my place to watched the sunset on my balcony and we couldn't stop talking.

We talked about everything, what we wanted in a relationship, he was single and had gotten divorced about a year ago. We talked about our goals, our vision for our coaching businesses, what we wanted to achieve in life, even our plans to have a family!

All the work I did with my coach, listening to my mentors, doing a manifestation, getting really clear about what kind of partner I wanted, and visualising it all, then letting go and trusting the universe, it all manifested into reality and this guy was the one I had asked for.

Later on I asked Raf what his version of our love story was.

He said that he was not looking for anyone, he wanted some stability because he had just gotten divorced, moved to Spain a few years ago and was setting up his coaching business with his partner and then Covid hit and everything changed for him.

Before we met, he said he listened to his intuition, because he also wanted to meet people who were conscious, spiritual entrepreneurs, and saw my book club online and wanted to join.

Raf is naturally an introvert and not inclined to go out and want to meet a lot of people often, but he said he felt drawn to going to my meetup in particular. He did resist it and question why it was this one he felt drawn to, and that was the first event he met Francesco, who told him about me being the host and founder of the group, and that I was sick with Covid that week.

Raf teaches and coaches a lot about following your intuition and walking your life path, so it was amazing and inevitable that the universe brought us together this way!

And since that day, we have been in a relationship together! As of this point of writing this book, we just celebrated our 2 year anniversary with a road trip to the Algarve, southern Portugal.

Raf is a balanced Alpha Male, who is highly emotionally intelligent, successful and stable and walks a similar life journey to mine, and we share the same vision of running a business together, to help people fulfil their greatest potential with abundance and prosperity in a community of like-minded people.

WHAT ARE SOME THINGS YOU WANT IN YOUR NEXT RELATIONSHIP?

CHAPTER 2. WHY DATING APPS DON'T WORK FOR HIGH LEVEL CAREER DRIVEN WOMEN

W hen I was single over a 5 year period after my divorce, I must have tried every dating app available out there. I thought I was taking lots of action, that it was just like sales - the more you date, the more people you meet, the greater chances you have of meeting someone special.

The reason why that approach doesn't work, is that it confuses you even more, and humans these days are not so great at making decisions, due to the overwhelm of options out there (leading to commitment-phobia - see next chapter).

Having TOO MANY choices often leads to over-analysing, constant DO-ing and not thinking enough or following your intuition, being in a state of BUSY-ness, and then you don't make a decision at all, or you make one and spend half the time doubting yourself, texting and calling your friends and leaving 20 minute voice messages analysing every move, every text message they sent you, trying to figure out what went wrong or what you should do next.

Dating apps are a great solution to meeting people in this online world, giving you a far greater reach and capacity and filter for meeting people than you could live in your own city.

But if you are a smart and savvy business owner or professional with not much time, you KNOW it takes a LOT of work to put together your profile, probably hours each day looking for matches, starting conversations, continuing conversations, making dates to meet in person, maintaining relationships, and half the time people may ghost you, unmatch you for no reason, stand you up on dates, or never call back after you've met, don't text back or block you.

WITH BUSINESS, YOU MUST HAVE SOME SORT OF STRATEGY, VISION AND MISSION STATEMENT. YOU MUST DO THE SAME WHEN LOOKING FOR A POTENTIAL LONG TERM PARTNER, IF YOU WANT TO HAVE AN EFFORTLESS, COMMITTED RELATIONSHIP.

Most people go onto these apps, with none of this in mind, and wonder how they get trapped wasting their hours each day with not much result.

The majority of people go there (myself included) thinking that a great profile, some good clear pictures of your face, with friends, a full body pic, doing activities that make you appear fun and attractive, are all you need to get a good match.

And most of the time it's true.

For most people out there.

But if you're one of the few entrepreneurs and professionals in the world that actually want to make an impact on the world through your work, you will want a partner who gives you inspiration and energy, not take away your focus through dramas, trauma and negativity.

During year 3, 4 and 5, I started getting frustrated at the kind of people I was meeting, wondering where all the people like me were - business owners, smart and successful people who also wanted a serious, committed relationship.

I even paid hundreds of dollars to join more 'exclusive' dating apps that promised high income earners, high net worth individuals, because I thought that there would be more serious, more people aligned to what I also wanted.

I realised the kind of potential partners I wanted were NOT on apps like these!

They had probably also gone through a similar process and quit those apps a long time ago.

What I realised eventually, was that you cannot outsource to an app, the real work you must first do - the first chapter in this book is about finding out what you want first, and most people who are on online dating apps have not done this inner work, don't know what they are looking for or what they want, and you will become one of thousands of lost and lonely singles drifting from chat to chat, profile to profile, no matter how many times you update your profile and try to stand out, get more matches etc

Like when you're building your business, you need to figure out who you will serve and what problem you can fix,

You can do the same with your values and creating a relationship manifesto - you immediately niche yourself and reduce the 95% of time wasting, speculating on the wrong types of people who are not in the same stage of the Love Journey as you are.

I thought that if I just found the right matching making, dating app, for other business owners and successful people, that they had done the hard work of selecting the right people, it would be much easier to meet the right one.

I found out that it's the same kind of lonely, frustrated people, but with more money.

I even met one guy who was probably one of the weirdest people I had ever met, so having money definitely doesn't mean you have good values, or even social skills!

Using dating apps can be part of your tactics, but you must first use a real STRATEGY, if you are to succeed.

You can also leave it to chance, to 'coincidence', to 'time will solve everything' kind of mindset, but if you're ambitious and keen to meet someone sooner rather than later, and low on time, then you are in the right place!

Please keep reading this book and I will show you the exact strategy I used to manifest and meet my partner Raf Adams, who has the same life purpose so we can grow and support each other on our life journeys.

WHAT DATING APPS/TACTICS HAVE YOU TRIED AND WHAT HAVE YOU LEARNED ABOUT YOURSELF?

CHAPTER 3. THE COMMITMENT PHOBIA EPIDEMIC

R ecently I had a networking call with another entrepreneur who helps people buy real estate in New York. She mentioned that her single female friends in New York were not having any success meeting men who wanted a committed stable relationship.

Another life coach in Sydney also mentioned the same thing, that Sydney was a hotspot of non-committed single people, not wanting to settle down and be with just 1 person.

Commitment phobia is a term used to describe a fear of commitment, particularly in romantic relationships. This fear can manifest in a number of ways, such as a reluctance to commit to a long-term relationship or a fear of getting married.

In recent years, there has been increasing awareness of commitment phobia as a widespread issue in the dating world, particularly among single people. Some experts have even described it as an "epidemic" due to the high number of individuals who struggle with this fear.

One of the main reasons for the prevalence of commitment phobia is the rise of hookup culture and casual dating. Many people have become accustomed to short-term flings and are hesitant to commit to a more serious relationship. This can be due to a fear of losing their independence or a desire to avoid the emotional risks that come with a committed relationship.

Additionally, some individuals may have experienced past traumas or relationship difficulties that have left them with a fear of intimacy and commitment. Others may struggle with self-doubt or insecurity, which can make it difficult to trust another person enough to commit to a relationship.

IT'S WORTH NOTING THAT COMMITMENT PHOBIA IS NOT ALWAYS A CONSCIOUS CHOICE OR A CHARACTER FLAW. IT CAN BE A LEGITIMATE FEAR THAT REQUIRES THERAPY OR OTHER FORMS OF SUPPORT TO OVERCOME.

Jane is in her late 40's and works as a fashion designer in Los Angeles. She is attractive, stylish, and enjoys going out to trendy restaurants and bars with her friends.

Despite her success in her career and social life, Jane has struggled to find a committed relationship. She has dated many attractive and successful men, but has found that they are often more interested in her looks and status than in getting to know her as a person.

Jane also has not been clear on her own values and what she is looking for in a partner, which has made it difficult for her to identify potential partners who align with her.

After a few failed relationships, Jane realizes that she needs to make some changes in order to find the kind of relationship she is looking for.

She takes a step back from the dating scene and spends some time reflecting on her own values and what she truly wants in a partner.

She also starts to be more intentional about the people she surrounds herself with, seeking out individuals who are kind, thoughtful, and share her values.

Through this process, Jane begins to attract different types of people into her life.

She meets someone who she initially writes off as not her type, but who turns out to be a great match for her in terms of personality, values, and goals. They start dating and eventually enter into a committed relationship.

Jane learns that sometimes the people we initially think are not our type can end up being the best matches for us, and that being true to ourselves and our values can help us find the right partner.

This is a common story for many successful entrepreneurs and professionals who are used to living in the yang energy, masculine, external world especially in large cosmopolitan cities, where our outward profile and ego is prized above all else, our reputation and what everyone else thinks about us becomes more important than being happy and enjoying our journey.

A great way to stop meeting commitment phobic people is to focus on your internal work, focusing on your values, life goals and vision for your life.

One exercise I have used at live speed networking events is to do the values exercise with everyone, and people form groups according to their values.

Once you have the same common values, then you can further narrow down your choices based on physical attraction, rather than looking for people with similar external and physical similarities.

Often your longterm partner may have an opposite personality and hobbies, but if you match on values, a future vision and the desire to be in a committed relationship to grow together, you will find your complimentary differences will help you achieve a happy and balanced relationship

ANOTHER WAY TO STOP THE COMMITMENT PHOBIA EPIDEMIC, IS TO CHANGE THE BALANCE OF POWER.

Women had the dating upperhand in the past century, and I believe that the collapse of traditional marriage in our society now, greatly impacts the way we date.

In many cultures, marriage was seen as a necessary step in adulthood and was often arranged by families. This meant that dating as we know it today, where individuals choose their own partners based on personal preferences, was not as common.

Instead, dating was often a more formal process with specific rules and expectations. For example, in some cultures, couples were expected to be chaperoned on dates or to only meet in public places. Men were often expected to be the initiators of courtship, and women were expected to be more passive.

Dating was also often seen as a means to an end, rather than an end in itself. That is, dating was a way for individuals to find a suitable partner for marriage, rather than a way to explore different relationships and experiences.

In some cultures, dating was also closely tied to social class and status. Individuals were expected to marry within their own social class, and dating outside of one's social class was often frowned upon.

This meant that dating was often a way for individuals to meet others within their own social circles, rather than a way to explore different communities and perspectives.

Overall, traditional marriage had a significant impact on how dating was conducted in the past. While dating as we know it today has evolved to become more casual and diverse, traditional marriage still plays a role in how some individuals approach dating and relationships.

So how do you make a commitment phobic person commit to you?

You don't!

You can't change a person, and someone who has all the potential, but isn't ready for a commitment, is NOT Mr Right.

And going for the short term pleasure, lust and satisfaction only makes this epidemic worse, as both males and females can get what they want physically with the click of an app, why bother putting in the hard work to find the right person for a long term relationship, when hooks and casual dating, friends with benefits are all 'normal' and 'acceptable' right now?

I remember my family being very upset with me when I told them I wanted to move in with my boyfriend (who became my ex-husband), I was in my late 20's and we had been dating for a few years already.

They held on to the traditional sense that you shouldn't live with your partner before marriage, probably more from a cultural shame perspective than from unwanted pregnancy or safety.

I didn't understand it back then, but as I grow older and wiser, I can see the wisdom of the traditional ways, why they wanted to keep women hidden away, unavailable and unaccessible.

As popular YouTube dating coach Matthew Hussey says, women need to portray themselves as high value, so men can feel confident they are choosing a valuable life partner.

I was a feminist for a long time, feeling objectified and vilified as an Asian female growing up in Australia, and I overcompensated for this imbalance by believing that women can act the same as men, that women SHOULD be behaving equally to men.

Now I know that feminism has changed the landscape of the gender balance and is the cause of the problems we have in relationships today.

WOMEN AND MEN ARE NOT EQUAL, WE ARE DIFFERENT, AND WERE DESIGNED TO COMPLIMENT AND EMPOWER EACH OTHER

Everyone has a masculine and feminine side and we have been living in a masculine dominant world both physically and mentally for centuries.

Matthew Hussey says the dating game was actually initiated by women in the past, dropping her handkerchief on the street in front of the man she liked, giving a subtle signal to him to make the first move, but in fact, she was the one making the first move.

In modern times, women feel like they don't have a lot of leverage in the dating game but in fact women have a lot more power than they think.

A successful, single entrepreneur or professional desires someone of equal or greater status to be their partner.

One book that talks about the desire for status is "Status Anxiety" by Alain de Botton. In the book, de Botton explores how the desire for status is a universal human characteristic and how it affects our lives, our relationships, and our societies. He argues that people are constantly striving for higher social status, and this desire can drive us to do great things, but it can also cause us to feel anxious, insecure, and unhappy. De Botton also examines the ways in which society reinforces the importance of status and suggests ways in which we can rethink our values to find greater fulfilment and meaning in life.

So if women (and men) were to use the status concept to their advantage, to make themselves highly desirable, and a way for a potential partner to elevate their status, doesn't the whole approach to dating change?

A very different dating strategy would be working on yourself, to define what makes you unique, what are your greatest strengths, what do you offer to a potential partner that would make them think you are the best deal around?

I find dating quite similar to business in this sense, your personal branding becomes very important, who you are and what you stand for communicates strongly to a potential partner.

If your personal brand, what you project to others is visionless, has unclear boundaries, lack of real values and full of emotional baggage, drama and traumas, does this help a potential partner elevate his status or not?

Perhaps this kind of branding would attract someone who is wanting that dramatic relationship, perhaps they have a saviour/martyr syndrome or dominant personality that wants to fix or change you? Or they psychologically derive some benefit or payoff that would make this kind of relationship attractive for them.

Would that be the kind of relationship you want?

WHAT KIND OF MEN HAVE YOU BEEN ATTRACTING? DO THEY WANT THE SAME THINGS AS YOU?

CHAPTER 4. HOW TO STAND OUT IN A CROWD OF 1000'S OF SINGLES

There is no one magical method to find your perfect partner, but might find comfort with the belief that there is no ONE perfect soulmate, there are MULTIPLE right people for you, at different stages of your life, and that each relationship is designed to teach you something about yourself and help you grow spiritually.

As a child I wondered how could people find someone who liked you back, like it was a 1 in a million chance!

As I grew older and learned from many different philosophies, and I chose the belief that our partners are there to help you grow, be a guide in your life journey. And when you outgrow them, you outgrow the relationship and it's time to part ways and find a new teacher.

So if you want a long term, life partner, you might want to look for a partner who also wants to grow and develop with you, and walk the journey of life together.

Most people will want to focus on making their online dating profile better, changing the photos, adding more photos, changing their bio, adding their instagram account etc...

Or going to event to meet people who have similar hobbies, going to speed dating, networking events, accepting blind dates from friends or going from bar to bar, club to club in the hopes of meeting someone attractive, interesting and exciting.

These are all temporary tactics and will give you the same results you are getting now.

As Albert Einstein said:

INSANITY IS DOING THE SAME THING OVER AND OVER AND EXPECTING DIFFERENT RESULTS

Most people will be focus on this, and you don't want the result of everyone else out there do you?

In business, the smartest thing is to do the opposite of what everyone else is doing, the counter-intuitive approach.

Everyone else changes on the outside and expects different results, and yes you may get some results, but they will be temporary. It's like pruning the leaves of an apple tree, hoping that it will grow oranges one day. You must plant a different type of seed and change your approach instead.

So if you want to stand out in a crowd of 100s of 1000s of other singles out there, and be noticed and connected with on the online dating apps, you might want to focus on the following first:

1. Focus on personal growth: Rather than solely focusing on finding a partner, focus on becoming the best version of yourself. This might involve meditating, looking after yourself, traveling, or engaging in activities that get you out of your comfort zone and challenge you. By investing in yourself, you'll not only become more diverse and attractive to potential partners, but you'll also gain a greater sense of self-worth and confidence.

2. Be authentic: It's important to be true to yourself when looking for a partner. Instead of trying to conform to societal norms or impress others, focus on being authentic and genuine in your interactions with potential partners. Let go of caring too much about what others think of you - remember that what they think about you is none of your business! This will help you attract people who appreciate and value you for who you truly are, and cut down the 90% who won't and will NEVER be right for you

3. Attend social events: Participating in social events such as parties, networking events, or community gatherings can be a great way to meet new people and expand your social circle. Let go of the idea of meeting new people to find a partner, instead go with the attitude of expanding your social circle and learning from different people. Your amazing, positive attitude will radiate warmth and attract people who want to help and connect with you on your love journey.

4.   Seek professional help: If you've been chronically single for a long time (4+ years) and are struggling to find a partner, it may be helpful to seek professional help from a therapist or dating coach. They can offer guidance and support as you navigate the challenges of dating and help you develop strategies to overcome any obstacles that may be standing in your way. If you'd like to have a chat with me, please book in a time to talk by clicking here)

WHAT MAKES YOU DIFFERENT & UNIQUE?

CHAPTER 5. HOW TO BE A HIGHLY DESIRABLE RELATIONSHIP MAGNET

D o you remember those people at school, at university, or at work, who are effortlessly popular, everyone wants to be friends with them, or be part of their group, be seen with them, hang out with them?

Those are magnetic people.

They have somehow mastered charm, fun and positivity into one package, and draw people to them like bees to flowers!

They are unconsciously competent in this highly useful skill in life.

One of my mentors talks about the 4 areas of competency in consciousness:

UNCONSCIOUS + INCOMPETENT	CONSCIOUS + INCOMPETENT
UNCONSCIOUS + COMPETENT	CONSCIOUS + COMPETENT

Some people who are naturally gifted with these incredible skills, or perhaps absorbed these growing up, learned from their parents and their environment around them when they were young.

A lot of us probably didn't grow up with these essential skills, and you might have been like me, shy, awkward and naive, not knowing what to do to attract the right people.

But as I grew older and started to grow and discover myself better, I started to naturally attract great partners who were interested in having a relationship with me.

I went from the yellow corner, drifted somewhere between the red and purple corners and finally mastered my magnetism to be firmly in the green corner.

The Unconscious + Incompetent means that you are not aware of what exactly attracts people, and you're not even aware it's something you can control.

The Conscious + Incompetent means that you are aware that changing your situation around dating is actually possible but you don't know exactly how to do it - hence why you are reading this book right now.

The Unconscious + Competent are those enviable people in the story I shared at the beginning of this chapter, the ones you know at work, from school etc who seem to be effortlessly popular and people just can't get enough of being around them!

And the Conscious + Competent - this is where you want to be, and you can definitely develop this in a shorter period of time than you think!

So how can you do this for yourself?

The great news is, being a magnetic, irresistible and highly desirable partner is completely learnable, and I can teach you exactly what I did.

STEP #2

After releasing my resistance blocks for my own personal life, I also did an exercise about values with my coach. I realised that I was not clear on my own values, so when I met someone who fit the physical characteristics, after a few weeks of dating I would discover that they actually weren't right for me and I would break it off as soon as possible (I was never one to waste time mulling things over!)

If you don't know your personal values, just choose your top 10 values, from a list of say 100 common values.

From that list of 10, give yourself about 5 mins to cut half of them down, so you end up with 5.

And from that 5, choose your top 3 values.

Sometimes you can group values together that are similar and choose the one that resonates with you most.

For example, my top values were personal growth, integrity and friendship. I wanted my partner to have similar values.

And I found that with my current partner, whom I met only a few months later, after doing this deep internal work.

When I do this exercise with my coaching groups, they suddenly recognise that it's better to have the same values and lifestyle than the same hobbies and interests - and I've often found that when people can only connect on the temporary, external features, they may have shorter relationships that don't grow and develop with them as they grow and change.

Some participants of my workshops ask how to introduce a conversation about their values with new potential partners, as it may seem too deep, too soon?

I always believe in a straightforward, direct approach, especially when it comes to relationships, because it gives space for each partner to choose and take action quickly, rather than wasting each other's time in a zone of indecision and uncertainty.

When I had the values conversation with my partner, it was after knowing him and talking to him for only a few hours.

Of course, the fact that we are both life coaches, helps a lot!

But if you're a smart, successful and savvy entrepreneur or professional, I'm sure you will also be looking for someone on your level, who doesn't have time to waste, and wants to invest yourself with someone as effortlessly and effectively as possible.

Having these deeper, meaningful quality conversations with people are often a great sign to know if someone is ready for a relationship too, and as you will find with 90% of people on certain dating sites, a lot of people just want to have fun and experiences, rather than grow and develop themselves within a relationship.

You can find out how to do this exact exercise as well as all the steps to help you to be in an effortless amazing committed relationship on my online course https:// www.entrepreneurlife.coach/love-journey-online-course

Another incredibly powerful way to become a desirable relationship magnet is to be on your life path.

My partner Raf Adams wrote a book called the Suited Monk, about how to be happy internally and still be successful externally, and also says:

BEING ON YOUR LIFE PATH IS MORE IMPORTANT THAN FINDING YOUR LIFE PURPOSE.

Because trying to find your purpose is a lifetime journey, and can be off-putting for a lot of people, like it's some grandiose Indiana Jones-style extreme quest, and a lot of people are too comfortable in their comfort zone, or their pain isn't big enough to take any action at all.

Being on a quest of some sort, having a direction in your life, being on a journey for some greater purpose than just making money, Netflix and chill on the couch or going out for drinks is often much more attractive to the entrepreneur and professional with a big vision and desire to make an impact on the world.

One dating coach on Youtube once made a video about how to attract women - and he says that women love to be taken on a journey.

And I admit it's true for myself. I would prefer a parter, or friends for that matter, who have a dream, an inspiration or some kind of movement they aspire to, because I'm like that myself.

Isn't it more fun to be around people who organise events, road trips, travel internationally, work with coaches and mentors, inspire you to grow and improve yourself, and push you to succeed in your work and your life?

Haven't you unconsciously attracted some relationship or friendship, job or client into your life, when you 'weren't looking'? Notice that you were probably in a very positive mindset, were happy, felt fulfilled and your life was at it's peak?

Only very rarely have I heard of people starting relationships when they were in a very difficult, negative place, and they are still together with their partner. For this situation, my perspective would be that this is their Dharma (they were meant to live this part of their journey), and they attracted the right partner to help them on this particular part of their journey, or this lifetime.

WHAT ARE YOUR KEY TAKEAWAYS?

CHAPTER 6. WHY YOU HAVEN'T MET YOUR PARTNER ALREADY

A bout the 3rd, 4th and 5th year of being single, I started to feel quite desperate, I wanted to have a family and my biological clock was ticking, and I started asking myself why I hadn't met the right one yet.

In the first few years I rationalised to myself that I had never been really single for the last 12.5 years, so it was a fantastic opportunity to find myself, explore and discover who I really was on my own, without having to make big decisions with someone else.

When I reflect back on those times, I was still enjoying my independence and freedom, and filled up my calendar with events, constantly busy, filling my mind with the routine of work, going to yoga, dance classes, maintaining friendships and going on dates with new guys, and there was never any time or space to be alone, be with myself and think about my situation.

I was trapped in a chronic singles pattern of 'DO, DO, DO', the constant busy-ness that I see in all my single friends now.

I heard in London that it can take 2-3 weeks to meet up with friends, as people book up their calendars so far in advance, just meeting for a coffee or drink is near impossible to fit in spontaneously.

One woman in her late 30's who came to a few of my live talks in Barcelona, always wanted to meet me, go for coffee and talk about coaching, but she was always so busy, even though she says she is looking to make the right decisions and change her life situation.

As you have been reading in this book, my life experiences have taught me to slow down, give myself space and time to think, meditate and ask for guidance that doesn't come from my own brain.

We put ourselves in our current situation because of our past programming, our software is out of date, and we keep trying to install new updates, when in fact we just need a complete upgrade of the operating system.

We aren't even aware of needing this mental, emotional and psychological upgrade because we don't have space for it in our busy lives.

If you're an ambitious DO-ER like me, taking a pause, stopping, stepping back, just doing NOTHING might be really challenging for you.

I know it was for me!

The years of living with every minute of time stretched out and filled with some activity, blocked me from hearing my inner guidance, so the Universe sent me signs to slow down.

YOUR PARTNER IS ALREADY THERE, WAITING FOR YOU, BUT YOU JUST CAN'T SEE THEM, BECAUSE YOU'RE NOT NOTICING THE SIGNS THE UNIVERSE/ DIVINE GUIDANCE HAS BEEN SENDING YOU

It makes sense to me now, why I waited so long to meet my Raf. He was still married up until a year before we met!

For years on my personal growth and spiritual journey, I had been practicing Tarot Card reading. Through my Mind Body Medicine diploma, I learned that everything is energy, and the cards are a physical representation of the message inside yourself, that your higher power wants to tell you.

When you choose a particular card, it's your intuition, matching the vibration of that particular card, (without seeing it with your eyes and choosing from your logical brain), and it's is a beautiful process that allows you to connect with your higher power and intuition and receive the right guidance you need at any time in your life.

I've been using the cards for over 10 years now, and about 7 of those years, the cards told me to 'Wait', 'Have Patience', 'Waiting Game', etc... and it was frustrating and I wondered if something was wrong and why it was taking so long!

Being an ambitious entrepreneur meant I was not used to leaving my future in someone else's hands, not being able to control the outcome was testing my patience!

But now when I pull cards for myself, I get cards about abundance, fertility, intuition, wisdom, accelerated motion, and that the fruits of my labour are available now, after sowing many different seeds and ideas.

Looking back, it made sense, the reading that my psychic healer friend Eve gave me before I left for Spain, the 5 year waiting period, and upon meeting Raf, discovering that he had been living in China and divorced his wife only a year before we met!

Was it a coincidence? I don't believe in coincidences anymore, I believe we are much more powerful than we think we are.

So if you haven't met your partner yet, please don't give up hope!

Please feel secure in the idea that your partner is on their growth journey, to become magnet, to become the person that you have envisioned in your Relationship Manifesto, and when you create space and listen to your inner guidance, it will confirm what actions will bring you closer together.

They are growing into the person they want to be, so they can attract someone amazing like you!

Or perhaps they are not ready for you yet, you may have other relationships in between, to teach you how to further refine your manifestation process, and each relationship will teach you something different about yourself.

And often they will be actions outside of your comfort zone (like moving to Barcelona!), and involve you to grow and change.

There are definitely several things you can do to make this process easier and faster, which I've documented from my 5 year experience of being single and how I made a huge breakthrough to have the relationship I have now,

You can check for new free trainings here on my social media: @michellechungcoach on Instagram

DESCRIBE WHAT YOUR CURRENT LIFESTYLE LOOKS LIKE - DO YOU HAVE SPACE FOR SOMEONE ELSE?

CHAPTER 7. HOW TO DETECT THE EARLY WARNING SIGNS OF PROBLEMATIC RELATIONSHIPS

If you live in a big city, you're probably more likely to meet people who have commitment issues, as highlighted in chapter 3, due to the huge range of options and lack of idealism towards marriage.

If you live in a small town, you may also have a problem of not having enough people to meet, exhausting availability of your location in your dating app (I know this has happened to me and people I knew when I was travelling to remote places, or live in smaller towns).

I remember one guy I was dating in Barcelona, he looked great on his profile, and when we met, he was sweet, chivalrous and attractive, had big plans for his new business and was warm and comfortable to be around.

But when we met for a second date, he couldn't commit a time to meet. I told him I would be at the museum and he couldn't tell me what time he would arrive.

Another friend told me she waited 90 minutes for a third date with one guy she really liked, and when he turned up, he just casually mentioned he knew she would be waiting anyway...

A lot of friends and clients had strict boundaries around these kinds of dating deal-breakers, and would cut people off, block them and move on quickly.

I've noticed that a better, more effective way, especially if you're a busy career professional and entrepreneur, is to rid yourself of these bad habits yourself.

The people you attract are a mirror of yourself.

If you have integrity issues, lack of boundaries, are 'too nice', thrive on dramas, complain about stuff all the time, bitch about other people, have unresolved past traumas or have an unnerving belief system around relationships, you need to seek help to sort these things out first, before you enter into a new relationship.

YOU ATTRACT WHO YOU ARE, AND IF YOU ARE NOT WORKING ON WHAT YOU BRING TO THE TABLE, YOU WILL ATTRACT PARTNERS WHO BRING THIS OUT OF YOUR SUBCONSCIOUS.

Relationships are not easy, yet their greatest advantage is highlighting things we like and don't like about ourselves.

For example, if you are someone who feels the need to fix all your partner's problems, or 'save' them constantly, what kind of person do you think you will be attracted to? A confident, independent person, or someone who is constantly in drama, needing your help to fix them?

I know a couple whose main problems are that she is too controlling, and that he is too laid back. He told me that what attracted him in the first place was her attention to detail, being a clean freak, because he was pretty casual and relaxed about those things.

The kind of relationship I'm recommending for busy, ambitious and successful people is a effortless relationship - but I'm not suggesting that you won't have problems or disagreements.

An effortless relationship is one of agreement, because you have decided to be together to support each other grow and help them see their blindspots, with patience and compassion.

In chapter 1, I share about my past relationships and the key pattern I had noticed was my being to masculine and critical. With this awareness, I worked on raising my feminine vibration and started doing less and listening to my intuition.

I recognised the problem with being in a relationship with boyfriend #3, the Spanish artist/fitness instructor, was that I needed a partner who was equally ambitious and inspire me to reach my full potential. If I had stayed in that relationship, I would be repeating my pattern and I would not have had the space to meet Raf.

STEP #3

You can also take a look at your belief system, it is often a huge cause of fights and relationship breakups, because if you don't have a similar belief system, it can be a huge warning sign.

It makes sense now, that traditional religions often advocated finding a partner from the same religion.

But of course you can do this in a secular way, and find someone who has the same mindset and belief system.

For example, one partner believes that all relationships are meant to be hard, difficult and stressful.

It's something they've probably picked up from their own parents growing up - fighting in front of their kids, raised voices, throwing things around, slamming doors etc.

Perhaps this method of communication is considered 'normal' for a person with this history and belief system.

And perhaps this person has developed a commitment phobia because subconsciously, they don't want to enter into this kind of relationship and tends to self sabotage before anything gets serious.

I was fortunate to change my belief system around relationships - when I was a child, it used to be 'how impossible it is to find someone who likes you back', to now: 'relationships are effortless and committed'. I was an unconscious competent. I had stumbled upon a way to change my belief system by accident, and hence all my relationships were effortless and committed.

Now my current beliefs are that relationships are effortless, growth focused and inspiring me to reach my fullest potential.

What are your beliefs around relationships?

DESCRIBE YOUR PAST RELATIONSHIPS, WHAT COMMON THEMES DO YOU SEE?

CHAPTER 8. HOW TO ATTRACT A STRONG, SUCCESSFUL, EMOTIONALLY MATURE MAN WHO IS READY TO COMMIT

D uring the time I was waiting for my visa, I was living life to the fullest while in Sydney, I joined the biggest Latin Dance schools in Sydney, and became part of a new group of single, 30-something friends who also loved dancing, I loved the latin music and dance community in Sydney.

One of friend from my new group of single friends, was a great guy who was starting his life coaching business, and we started dating, and he said something very interesting to me:

'YOU'RE AN ALPHA FEMALE, YOU NEED AN ALPHA MALE'

It was a huge revelation for me, I had never heard myself described in that way before!

I never considered myself an Alpha Female; my family would have described me as stubborn, highly independent, rebellious and too 'Aussie' (being the youngest of my family and the easiest to adapt to the western, anglo Saxon culture), whereas my friends would have described me as confident, courageous, fearless and independent.

This comment gave me a clue about the types of men I had attracted in my past, and I saw a common thread - they were a lot less ambitious than I was and I guess you could say that I 'wore the pants' most of the time.

I knew that men were attracted to me because I was smart and independent, and wasn't needy or nagging, but what kind of man did I want?

I realised upon reflecting on my past relationships, if I was to attract someone more masculine than me, an Alpha Male, I would need to reduce my masculine energy by increasing my feminine vibration.

I deduced that overpowering, aggressive Alpha Females would only attract Beta males, who were more feminine and submissive in order to compliment each other and avoid a power struggle.

And no woman wants to be publicly labelled an Alpha Female, it alludes to aggression, autocratic, over powering - all negative, derogatory and un PC.

And if I was to attract an Alpha Male I would need to tone down my masculine characteristics by increasing my feminine vibration.

I didn't want to repeat my past relationships where I was more ambitious than they were, because I recognised that either I got bored and I wanted more from life, to reach my greatest potential and make an impact on the world before I left the planet.

I felt like my past relationships did not give me a nurturing structure to grow and discover my inner zone of genius, and I wanted my partner to be my equal or on a higher level emotionally, spiritually and financially so I could be inspired and have a teacher, guide and mentor within my relationship, and finally receive instead of constantly giving and leading and guiding others around me.

EXPLORING THE MASCULINE VS FEMININE

Being in a relationship where I had to make all the decisions all the time was so exhausting - you could say that an Alpha Male would take the initiative and leadership in a relationship and his partner could just trust, feel safe and accept his care, and this was something I was missing and craving in a relationship.

During my 3rd year being single, I had started following UK's top dating coach Matthew Hussey, after my dear friend Priscilla from my dancing group introduced me to his content.

He said that women want to be led in a relationship

Another online dating coach said that women want to be taken on a journey, and the relationship needed to have leadership by the masculine side.

So I guess this works in LQBGT relationships too, although I'm not an expert here, I have alpha female lesbian friends who are more masculine and would probably take on the masculine side of the relationship.

In a later chapter I'll go into more detail about the masculine feminine balance and how to master this so you can attract the right partner for you in this part of your Love Journey.

So how to raise my feminine vibration?

Through my studies in Kinesiology and Mind Body Medicine, getting in touch with your body, your intuition and being in a state of receiving are all ways of increasing your feminine vibration.

Activities like yoga, dancing, meditation, or anything creative like drawing painting etc were recommended.

So I pursued my passion for Latin dancing, I went to a few classes every week to improve my Bachata, Kizomba (not to be confused with the gym fitness Zhumba) and Zouk, and I fell in love with expressing myself through dance.

One of the main reasons I loved Latin dancing in particular was the concept of masculine and feminine energy.

I remember one of my first classes was Kizomba, a friend from my Kinesiology and Mind Body Medicine course had introduced it to me soon after I broke up with my ex-husband, to get me out of the house and be more social again.

I was partnered with a stranger, a nice looking young guy from Poland who immigrated to Sydney.

I was struggling to see the dance teacher, and follow the steps, and he just said to me, 'You don't need to see the steps, just follow me.'

This kind of comment at that time freaked me out a little, letting go of control for an Alpha female was a little unnerving!

PARTNER DANCING IS MASCULINE TO FEMININE COMMUNICATION, FROM LEADER TO FOLLOWER

It's also quite common for women to be leaders in the dancing world, once they have mastered the follower steps, because there are far more women who love dancing than men! Hint to all the men out there who want to meet more women in a safe, fun environment!)

If the dance goes badly, it's generally accepted to be the fault of the leader, because he/she did not communicate the dance moves clear enough in a way that his partner/follower could understand it.

The leader communicates through body language, the amount of pressure and position of his/her torso arms and legs to move their partners around in tempo appropriate with the music.

It is also the follower's responsibility to know the basic dance movements and to learn how to be follow, how to listen and feel for the body signals her partner is giving.

I felt like latin dancing was a huge personal growth program, learning how to use my body, getting in touch with my feminine side, allowing myself to be led instead of trying to control everything so I could focus on receiving energy from my partner instead.

THE COMMITMENT THING AGAIN

No one wants to be locked into a bad deal. It's a simple negotiation, everyone wants a win-win deal

Everyone has a masculine and feminine side within yourself, and even same sex relationships will have a masculine feminine balance too.

For strong, more masculine women like myself, who are more dominant or successful than most people generally, it can be intimidating for a man who is not also dominant and strong.

And you don't want to have an overly aggressive male partner either, they will probably attract a hyper feminine, submissive female.

Many men are not wanting commitment with women if they are too much like their best friends, women need to offer a positive vision of the future with aligned goals, if they are looking for a committed relationship.

Too often, women are too relaxed about what they want, or way too rigid, and not able to offer an inspiring scenario of what a potential future with them would look like.

Once you balance your feminine with your masculine, you will be better able to attract men who are also emotionally intelligent, stable and want the same thing you do - and trust me, they are out there, waiting to be found by you!

DESCRIBE YOUR MASCULINE VS YOUR FEMININE SIDES?

CHAPTER 9. THE UNDESIRABLE LOSERS - ALPHA WOMEN AND POOR MEN

A very interesting conversation with a successful, married business owner on Linked In led to some very deep insights, which ended with the sentence 'Alpha Women and poor men are unfortunately an undesirable type of partner when you're single.'

I'm sure this statement would ruffle a lot of feathers in the single world out there - indignant cries of 'that is so politically incorrect and stereotyping!'

But let's dissect this statement from a biological point of view

What my Linked In contact probably meant was - there is nothing wrong with being either of these, but it's a lot harder for you to find a partner.

Let's start with the Alpha Woman.

While researching for this book, I've discovered that calling a woman and Alpha, is not desirable, can be offensive and derogatory.

Why?
Perhaps simply that Alpha implies dominance, hierarchy, aggression, autocratic and dictatorial, and no one wants to be associated with that.

I've also been told in the past, that I'm an Alpha woman, and I've always made more money than my partners in the past too.

What is it about an Alpha woman that makes her undesirable to the average male?

I asked ChatGPT for some feedback:

While some men might find confidence, assertiveness and ambition attractive and appealing, others might find them intimidating or emasculating. This can be due to societal norms and gender stereotypes that associate masculine traits with dominance and femininity with submissiveness. Therefore, some men might feel threatened or uncomfortable around women who exhibit traditionally masculine traits.

As mentioned before about masculine and feminine energy, the average man is more attracted to a woman who displays more typically feminine traits, which can conflict with the feminist idealism.

It goes back to the traditional stereotype of a man's pride being connected to his ability to earn and look after his family, and with feminism came the change of power and income provided by both sides of a relationship instead.

A lot of successful women I've coached are Alpha women, and they craved freedom and independence above all else, which can be difficult for a partner who wants to feel needed.

In fact these women were very hesitant to get into relationships if they felt their freedom would be compromised in any way, preferring not to be in a relationship at all.

Now what about the Poor Man?

When I was on the dating apps for 5 years while I was single in my late 30's, I would meet men who told me that they were incredibly wary of the gold-digging women on dating apps who wanted them to pay for all their dates and insisted on paying half each, to test the potential of a future partner.

And once I was chatting with some women friends with Russian heritage, and they informed me that dating was a huge industry, where some women would intentionally arrive to a date without their wallet, expecting their date to pay for them.

Who pays on the date has always been a huge debate, and one Polish friend mentioned his mother always insisted that he allow his dates to pay half, as women were earning money now, so they should contribute.

No matter what the argument is, a man or a woman who is unemployed or purposeless, is highly undesirable romantically right?

Even though a lot of women are capable of paying for and looking after themselves, deep down we all want our partner to look after us, emotionally, physically and perhaps even financially - a throwback to the survival scenario if we ever have kids and raise a family, would all the responsibility fall on just one partner, or could both share the duties in a balanced way?

And many women on dating apps search for men who are financially stable, have a good job, and can offer some stability and security.

I asked Raf once 'Does it matter if a guy doesn't know how to drive?' To which he answered yes of course it does! It affects the masculine pride and the ability to see him as someone who is responsible and capable of looking after himself and for others.

I've also dated some men who didn't drive, didn't own a car, rode a bicycle everywhere, and I told myself that it didn't matter, it was superficial, but in the end I chose to be with someone who was financially stable, well travelled and who I could learn and grow with, which was more aligned to the stage of life I was in.

Being financially unstable, unemployed are undesirable to a potential partner as it shows a lack of solid foundation and security, and everyone wants security!

It also may point to a potential lack of self worth, if a person is not going for the best career or lifestyle, do they think they are not capable, worthy or possible for them?

As mentioned in a previous chapter, we all subconsciously desire to increase our status in the world, move 'up' from our current situation, even if it's a simple thing like having more free time to exercise, relax in the quiet, or if it means expanding our business and careers.

And a man's status may be the main, obvious priority for some women, but most women will prefer their partner of equal status and financial stability.

WHAT ARE YOUR KEY TAKEAWAYS?

CHAPTER 10. THE MAJOR PROBLEM IN RELATIONSHIPS TODAY- WHAT MEN & WOMEN REALLY WANT ARE DIFFERENT

W hen I first started dating my partner Raf, he introduced a book to me, and as I loved personal growth books, I bought it online straight away. He recommended I read it because it was about relationships and how men and women need different things.

Love & Respect is a book written by Dr. Emerson Eggerichs that explores the fundamental principles of successful relationships, with a particular focus on marriages.

The book proposes that men and women have different needs in relationships, and that these needs can be boiled down to two essential elements: love and respect.

According to Eggerichs, men primarily crave respect from their partners, while women primarily desire love.

The book outlines practical strategies for meeting these needs and building a strong, healthy, and fulfilling relationship.

Love & Respect is a highly influential book that has helped countless couples improve their marriages by providing them with valuable insights into the unique dynamics of male-female relationships.

And my good friend Chelsea Joy Arganbright, an expert on how the masculine and feminine interacts with each other, recommended the books, "For Women Only" and "For Men Only" by Shaunti Feldhahn.

In "For Women Only," Feldhahn argues that men primarily crave respect in their relationships, while women desire to feel cherished and desired.

Conversely, in "For Men Only," she discusses how men can best meet the emotional needs of their female partners by understanding their desire for love, affection, and emotional connection.

When I heard about these concepts of 'Unconditional Respect' for men, I could not understand this.

I thought respect was earned.

It's common to know that unconditional love is normal, acceptable, as parents love their children unconditionally.

But unconditional respect was a completely new concept for me.

What if they do something 'wrong' or something I don't agree with? Do I just be silent and not voice my opinions? It was a very controversial topic for me.

Showing someone unconditional respect can be challenging, as it involves treating others with respect even when they may not deserve it or when you disagree with them.

Some ways to show unconditional respect include:

1. Refraining from judgment: Avoid making assumptions or passing judgment on others, and try to approach conversations with an open mind and a willingness to learn.
2. Practicing active listening: Show that you are engaged in what the other person is saying by actively listening and asking questions to show that you are interested in their perspective.
3. Using respectful language: Speak to others in a kind and courteous manner, using phrases such as "please" and "thank you" when appropriate, even if you disagree with their views.
4. Being empathetic: Try to put yourself in the other person's shoes and understand their perspective, even if you don't agree with it.
5. Avoiding personal attacks: Refrain from attacking the other person's character or using derogatory language, even when you strongly disagree with their views.
6. Honoring their boundaries: Respect other people's personal space and privacy, and avoid doing anything that makes them feel uncomfortable or violated.

I asked my partner about this concept, unconditional respect. He says that if a woman shows respect to her partner, he man feels significant and that he's on the right track, he says it's more to do with biological instinct, to lead and look after his family.

That's why there are major problems in modern relationships, the ancient concept of showing respect in more important than love for men.

It reminds me of traditional marriages, perhaps in generations before ours, before feminism, before women had the power and ability to work, run businesses, have children on our own and be equal members of society.

I find it interesting to note that a lot of traditional rules for marriages are still quite relevant today, but must be interpreted for a modern era, to work with the modern, independent woman.

Perhaps there are gems of wisdom from our ancestors that would be worth re-looking at, if we are to make our modern relationships work.

It was obviously much easier for me to see the point of view of the woman, and I listed some ways that women commonly feel loved and appreciated include:

1. Affectionate touch: Many women feel loved and cherished when their partner shows them physical affection, such as hugging, cuddling, or holding hands.
2. Quality time: Spending quality time together, whether it's going on dates, taking walks, or simply having meaningful conversations, can make a woman feel loved and cherished.
3. Acts of service: Doing things to make a woman's life easier or more enjoyable, such as cooking dinner, running errands, or doing household chores, can show her that she is valued and appreciated.
4. Verbal affirmations: Telling a woman how much she is loved and appreciated, and expressing gratitude for the things she does, can help her feel valued and desired.
5. Gifts: Giving thoughtful gifts, whether it's a small token of affection or a grand gesture, can make a woman feel cherished and special.

6. Physical attraction: Many women feel desired when their partner shows them physical attraction, such as complimenting their appearance or initiating intimacy.

These tips can be commonly distinguished in the book 'The Five Love Languages', about the way we show and receive love can be different for different people.

Did you see this kind of Love and Respect concept in your parents relationship growing up?

Do you see it in any happy relationships around you?

HOW DO YOU WANT TO EXPERIENCE LOVE IN YOUR NEXT RELATIONSHIP?

CHAPTER 11. SHOULD YOU FRIEND-ZONE HIM OR DATE HIM?

R af and I were watching the Netflix series Suits (we love cuddling on the couch in the evenings and watching clever movies and inspiring series), and Raf pointed out something really important, and something I've subconsciously done myself when talking to men.

The main character Mike Ross was talking to his love interest Rachel Zane, and she wasn't so sure about him yet, even though she thought he was brilliant and witnessed him slowly earning the respect and admiration from their colleagues and bosses in their law firm, Mike had clearly shown interest in dating Rachel since they first met, but she wanted to put her career first, and not get distracted from her goal of becoming a lawyer in the firm.

Raf pointed out the behaviour of Mike, that he was close to getting friend-zoned if she lost respect for him.

Mike was starting to behave in a way subservient to Rachel's super independent and smart character, acting like a friend rather than a well-matched potential partner.

It doesn't mean that men have to be domineering, aggressive or autocratic to gain attention and respect, but men should NOT allow themselves to be in a position of perceived weakness or low standing, in a way that shows he could not be a sturdy emotional, financial and physical status.

If he starts behaving in a way that disrespects himself, or loses his dignity, women (especially strong, independent successful women) will instantly lose hope for him as an equal, potential partner.

Being vulnerable is a completely different thing, and is attractive to everyone, when being authentic, honest and coming from a desire to be open and learn from the situation.

Once I had a zoom meeting with a single businessman who said he did really well talking to women, but would get annoyed because the women he liked always insisted on bringing a chaperone and would friend zone him immediately.

He wondered what he was doing that was giving off the friend zone vibe.

As I mentioned earlier, I have also subconsciously friend zoned men when I knew they were of a lower status in success, finances, emotional intelligence and had less testosterone than I did!

In today's world, we have an imbalance of masculine and feminine energy, and as women gain more masculine habits and behaviours, men have compensated by becoming hyper masculine (Andrew Tate's Alpha man) or more feminine, perhaps like this man.

He said that he had great sexual prowess, but it was clear he was not promoting this effectively, and he was also not promoting his capability for being a leader or someone who could look after someone other than himself (he didn't have a stable foundation or home life).

Women biologically look for men with more testosterone than themselves, (or perhaps an imbalanced Alpha woman would look for a man she could dominate), to ensure survival for her children, should she want them.

Women lose interest in men who are not emotionally or financially intelligent, or still act like kids who need someone to look after them.

I had a Korean beautician in Sydney, and she mentioned that not many Korean women wanted to be with Korean men, it was epidemic!

She said that no one wanted to feel like they were stuck in the past century where women were not valued or empowered and only expected to be an adequate housewife.

As women were becoming successful in their careers, they wanted men who valued and respected their choices, and not only expected them to be at home, looking after their men and their kids.

A lot of women today wish they could meet a man who is stable, secure, responsible and mature, and it is a known fact that women mature faster than men, and perhaps dating older men is one solution, but this is definitely not a guarantee.

The issue here, is that women will naturally be more picky than men, biological we have a lot more to lose than men, it is in our nature to search for the most suitable biological match for the survival of our DNA, and for men they seem to have a lot more options these days as people don't wait for marriage before becoming intimate.

I heard the phrase once before that 'men don't know how to be men anymore' and to that I say:

IT'S UP TO US WOMEN TO CHANGE THAT. WE HAVE A LOT MORE POWER THAN WE BELIEVE

We need to treat men with respect and they will rise up and reach their full potential, with our respect and partnership.

As written in Napoleon Hill's 1937 classic 'Think and Grow Rich', the love of women makes men great, that men will discover and achieve their zone of genius with the partnership of a woman who believes in him.

Women need to gently support men, to allow them to become the man he needs to become.

Women nowadays are used to doing everything ourselves, we are independent and successful more than the generations of our mothers and grandmothers.

If a woman likes a man and sees his potential but he may not be quite 'there' with you yet, before friend zoning him too quickly, (not talking about the ones who are commitment phobic and not ready for a committed relationship, pls see earlier chapter), give him a chance, he may not be perfect right now, but you can support him in becoming the best version of himself (so he can lead, support and be emotionally available for you).

Women tend to naturally see the potential in their men, which is why we also sometimes try to push them too hard, or get impatient when they are still trying, and we need to be supportive and respectful when they fail (not 'if' they fail, we ALL fail in the beginning when are learning and growing)

An important thing to note is that in the beginning of a new relationship, women need to stay in our own boundaries, we shouldn't emotionally surrender ourselves until it's clear if you're both invested into the relationship, otherwise women can get in too deep, giving too much of ourselves, trying to help, save or fix the man, which is NOT the ideal relationship (see earlier chapter about the Love Journey, or watch the training at www.michellechungcoach.com)

When there is mutual desire for a relationship, even though women might feel he is not quite on the same level with her yet, if she believes in his potential, and he is interested in exploring this and growing with her, it could be an extremely rewarding and loving relationship.

As the relationship grows, she can suggest and guide him on how how she prefers the relationship to go or how she wants to be supported and guided herself, it will help the man to grow into his fullest potential, and she can have the fulfilling, loving and committed relationship she desires.

He may feel insecure, if he can't manage a situation in the relationship, so women need to be supportive and allow him to make his own mistakes and grow and learn from them, and not push him too fast or sternly if things don't go smoothly.

If she supports him on how to behave in certain situations, her man grows, and she stays within her boundaries, asserting herself emotionally and being the pillar for growth in their relationship.

So It's really important that women are really aware and firm of our own boundaries.

A great example of this, Raf was helping me write this chapter by sharing his own story of his past relationship.

When Raf was in his 20's and was becoming successful in his career, he met a woman 8 years older, and were together in a relationship for 5 years.

Raf says she was way above his league, she was very much into personal growth and had done a lot of work on herself already when they met, and Raf was still highly unconscious and focused on his career success.

He says with her support and guidance, he was able to grow in their relationship, because she saw his potential and was willing to be part of his journey.

Because she believed in him and was willing to be patient and let him make his own mistakes and learn, eventually he caught up to her emotional intelligence and personal development and eventually decided to be a life coach himself.

They eventually split up due to her insecurities and other problems and she stopped growing so Raf outgrew her over the course of their relationship.

So if you're a woman looking for an equal partner to inspire you and grow with, you can also widen your potential partner prospect list by considering some men you might have friend-zoned because they are not quite there with you yet.

The most important thing you need to be sure of, is if he wants to grow and develop himself or not, if he is READY to walk the journey together with you.

He will be keen to be with you and ready to commit, and just requires your support and patience for him to reach his full potential and grow into the man he is meant to be

DESCRIBE HOW YOUR IDEAL PARTNER BEHAVES IN YOUR NEXT RELATIONSHIP?

CHAPTER 12. ALL THE GOOD ONES ARE TAKEN, THE LEFTOVERS ARE DAMAGED!

A lot of strong, single, successful women are wondering 'Are there any good men left out there? All the good ones are taken already!'

A lot of single women and men have had this thought, if you live in a big city where there are a lot of other singles or even if you live in a smaller city with less options.

You might look around you sigh, because you may have done a lot of work on yourself already, personal growth, therapy, counselling, dating, matchmaking and still haven't found anyone close to where you are in your life.

The solution here, as I was discussing with Raf, is there are 2 options for women looking for suitable partners, who are as successful, emotionally intelligent and have done a lot of inner work already

1. Women must realise that this is a huge limiting belief. The idea that there are 'NONE' out there is only a belief. He is definitely out there for you, there are just a few steps in the way to being together, and those can be your subconscious resistance (as mentioned in earlier chapters), that stops you from meeting him. You need to change your

belief to one where he is on his way, he is also on his journey for growth and becoming the one you desire most.

2. Patience - a major mistake we make as women is being too impatient or forceful, because we have our biological clock, or perhaps we want to spend our best years with someone sooner rather than later. As explained in the previous chapter, it's important to also acknowledge that perhaps your soulmate is someone you've already met, but haven't seen as a potential partner because you're expecting him to be a certain way already.

As a participant in my last online webinar mentioned, it seems that a lot more women are doing personal growth work, therapy and counselling to grow and develop themselves, so we may be a little further on the conscious, spiritual journey and don't find as many men who are there with us.

My response was about patience, as an entrepreneur, I'm used to getting things done, and move on quickly, and not used to waiting around.

I share the story about being single for 5 years, getting feedback from my tarot cards about having to wait, be patient and things are coming up ahead.

I realise now, after meeting Raf, why I had to wait so long!

Raf was married until a year before we met, he was also on his own spiritual path, had moved to Spain from China and was going through his own life journey.

If you can keep in mind, that finding your partner is a spiritual process, it's meant to come at the right time, and provide a learning and growth experience for the exact thing you need right now, you can trust the universe (or higher power, God, etc) will deliver the right person to you when you're ready.

Learning to trust and let go is a huge thing for us entrepreneurial women, we must raise our feminine vibration and use the feminine energy more so we can rebalance ourselves and allow ourselves to receive what we want, instead of pushing and forcing and using masculine energy.

CHAPTER 13. HOW TO MAINTAIN YOUR FREEDOM AND LIFESTYLE AND STILL BE IN A SERIOUS RELATIONSHIP

A few clients I've coached were most afraid of losing their freedom and lifestyle, and it blocked them from being in a serious, committed relationship.

Most of them had been in traumatic past relationships that still haunted them, even though they said they were ready to be in a new relationship, they hadn't come to terms with some emotional baggage that hadn't been dealt with.

One client used the **Resistance exercise** to uncover this deep seated blockage, and when she recognised that her marriage had made her feel trapped, she was emotionally available to choose freedom as one of her top values instead.

Losing your freedom and lifestyle was the #1 factor that stopped these successful business owners and professionals from putting themselves out there, or if they were dating, they would subconsciously choose partners who would not be a right fit long term, because they were so fearful of losing the lifestyle and freedom that single life afforded them.

Here are some practical tips to maintain your current single freedom and lifestyle and still have the benefits of a effortless, committed relationship:

1. Communication: Communication is key in any relationship, and it's especially important when it comes to balancing your freedom and lifestyle with your partner's needs and expectations. Be honest and open with your partner about your goals, values, and boundaries, and listen to their needs and concerns as well. This can help you establish a shared understanding of what you both want from the relationship and how you can support each other's individual goals and desires.

2. Set boundaries: Boundaries are essential for maintaining your sense of freedom and autonomy in a relationship. Be clear about what you're comfortable with and what you're not, and be willing to negotiate and compromise as needed. This might involve setting limits on your time, space, or activities, or establishing rules around communication and privacy.

3. Maintain your interests: It's important to continue pursuing your own interests and hobbies even when in a serious relationship. This can help you maintain your sense of identity and independence, and can also make you a more interesting and attractive partner. Make time for the things you love, and encourage your partner to do the same.

4. Practice self-care: Taking care of yourself is essential for maintaining your physical, emotional, and mental well-being. Prioritize self-care activities such as exercise, meditation, or therapy, and communicate with

your partner about the importance of these practices in your life.

5. Plan together: Planning and scheduling time together can help you balance your individual needs and desires with your relationship. This might involve setting aside specific date nights, taking turns planning activities, or finding shared interests that you both enjoy.

Ultimately, maintaining your freedom and lifestyle while being in a serious relationship requires a balance of communication, boundaries, self-care, and shared planning.

By being honest and open with your partner, setting clear boundaries, pursuing your own interests, practicing self-care, and planning together, you can create a fulfilling and sustainable relationship that honours both your individuality and your commitment to each other.

Doing the **Relationship Manifesto** exercise is a really important way to maintain your freedom and lifestyle, it was the key element for me to create my ideal relationship because I also valued a lifestyle different from most people, and helped guide me to meet someone who also felt the same way.

When I did this work for myself, I created a manifestation story, of exactly how I wanted my relationship to be like, what my partner and I would do, what we would accomplish together, and our vision.

I remember reading it again 2 years later and was amazed at how accurate it was, like I had read my future relationship, everything was pretty much how I had described it in the **Relationship Manifesto!**

It helped create a new mindset of hope and possibility, and trust that the universe conspires to bring everything you want to your reality.

As we get older and more set in our ways, a lot of us don't want to have the same kind of relationship as when we were younger.

And it doesn't make sense either.

Our relationships will always be about our growth and discovery, but as we mature, perhaps we need to seek partners who share your values of freedom and having an amazing lifestyle, enjoying the result of everything you've worked so hard for in your 20's and 30's.

DESCRIBE HOW YOU COULD USE THE 5 TIPS ABOVE IN YOUR NEXT RELATIONSHIP?

CHAPTER 14. HOW TO MOVE FORWARD FROM HERE - ARE YOU READY?

Whenever I tell people I help business owners and professionals find love, they always tell me what a great niche it is, saying that Barcelona is a city full of single people, and I can imagine every major city in the world also full of singles looking for love.

In my live and online talks about conscious dating and meeting great quality people, I share my model on the journey of love, how people move from childhood to young adult, where you learn your beliefs and witness role models and these form the basis for your early relationship. Because you were raised in a dependent mindset (depending on your parents for food, shelter, love etc), believing you need someone else for something is natural and automatic.

I reference Stephen Covey's book 'The 7 Habits of Highly Effective People' because he mentions the states that relationships go through, and I've incorporated this into my own model The Love Journey.

However, there are many single people in the different stages of the Love Journey, and most are in the Dependent relationship stage and not necessarily wanting to be in the kind of relationship I'm proposing in this book - an effortless, committed relationship, or an Inter-Dependent relationship.

Most people are still too hooked into the everyday norms, relying on alcohol, Netflix, emotional eating, hookup dates, overworking and other ways too numb themselves from listening to what they really want, or are too afraid or not ready to open their hearts and change direction.

The chapters in this book will help you understand where you are in your Love Journey, and decide if you're ready to be in an effortless, committed relationship.

NOT EVERYONE IS READY, OR PERHAPS LOOKING FOR A SHORT TERM, WARM BODY FOR WINTER IS A MUCH EASIER WAY TO APPROACH DATING AND RELATIONSHIPS.

One client I worked with, sent me a text six months later, apologising because she had gone AWOL, that she had fallen in love!

She had gone travelling out of the USA, and had always wanted to go to Africa, and there she said she met a man who was the most mature, intelligent man she had ever met!

After our coaching, she had unblocked a lot of beliefs around not being able to find anyone, because her subconscious belief was that it was NOT POSSIBLE anyway, so her reality was giving her, her beliefs.

Her biggest breakthroughs and results were that she finally had HOPE again, that someone is there for her, if it's not this guy, perhaps it's the one after, as she grows and develops herself, and rediscovers trust, hope and faith in her love journey.

Through the specific exercises we did together, she transformed her mindset around love and relationships, because your physical reality is a consequence of your thoughts, beliefs and behaviours.

True transformation is simple, but we always overcomplicate things, and if you follow a specific method that other people have already followed, you will get results for yourself too.

Another client was looking for love, and had an on-off relationship with a man, and she was not sure if he was the right one. She wanted someone who was also interested in her hobbies, and who was more romantic.

Through the coaching work we did together, she realised that the hobbies and being romantic were not as important as her values of growth and stability, and this relationship already gave her what she really needed, and the other parts she could work out with him. She decided to stay together with him and now enjoys a relationship where they both grow together, have improved their communication and now planning a family of their own.

I hope you found this book valuable and take action on using some of the tools in this book as a guide to help you move through your dating experiences with more ease and effortlessness.

... and if you're looking for a better way to meet men offline & in-person, you can check out this free 10 minute training that hundreds of women have been raving about, because they realised they have been choosing the wrong men all along!

Check it out at: www.manifestyoursoulmateinperson.com

See you on the inside!

Michelle Chung

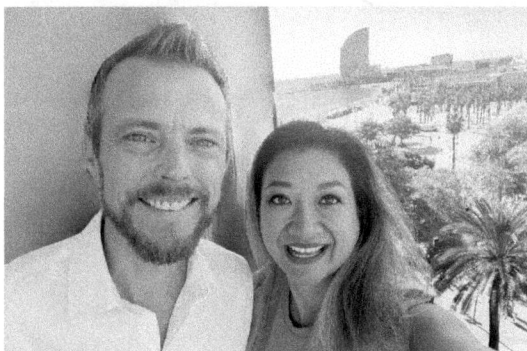

ABOUT THE AUTHOR

Michelle Chung is a certified life coach with the John Maxwell Team, popular speaker with live events and online events with 100's of attendees, a trained kinesiologist and mind body medicine specialist, with an 18 year career in product design and development in manufacturing across the fashion, footwear, kitchenware and beauty sectors.

Michelle specialises on finding love for single business women and professionals and has been in the personal growth industry since 2008.

She continues to follow her life purpose together with her life partner Raf Adams, who is also an executive coach, speaker and trainer. They share the same vision of working with entrepreneurs and professionals to find their true path and reach their greatest potential through their careers and businesses.

For more content, products and services, please go to:

www.michellechungcoach.com

www.ingramcontent.com/pod-product-compliance
Lightning Source LLC
Chambersburg PA
CBHW062144020426
42334CB00020B/2502